"I love *Space Between the Stones*. It is dc
deeply spiritual—living poetry that in
the mystery, the ordinary, and the beauty and wonder
of life."

—Bob Stahl, co-author of five books on mindful living,
including *A Mindfulness-Based Stress Reduction Workbook,
Living With Your Heart Wide Open*, and *Calming the Rush
of Panic*

"Zen poet meets Earth goddess. Kai's writing is graced
by a sense of calm and spaciousness and rooted in an
earthy mix of sensuality, playfulness, and wisdom."

—Mary Reynolds Thompson, CAPF, CPCC, author
of *Reclaiming the Wild Soul*

"Come to these pages and find refuge—from lives
made too busy, from the incessant drumbeat of bad
news, from the lure and grip of technology, from
endless distraction and interaction. Here amongst
words so carefully and elegantly chosen we can be
reminded of our primal connections—to a sometimes-
forgotten place inside and to nature in all its forms.
This exquisitely crafted collection deserves to be
savored again and again."

—Michael Ableman, farmer and author of *On Good
Land, Fields of Plenty*, and *Street Farm*

"If you're seeking a deeper connection with nature,
Spirit, or creativity, Kai Siedenburg's wonderful book
Space Between the Stones is an inspiring and insightful
resource. These evocative poems and simple practices
invite us into a direct and open-hearted relationship
with Earth and Spirit that can sustain us and give us
hope in these challenging times."

—Linda Buzzell, co-editor, *Ecotherapy: Healing with
Nature in Mind*

"Each poem is better than the next, and resonates with her unique voice and mastery of lightness, surprise, humor, and profound wisdom… Her words breathe life into ink on a page; and her poems and practices offer connection, hope, and useful ideas to help us navigate through each day… *Space Between the Stones* is written in a language of wonder, a true gift for these changing times and world."

—From the Foreword by Ilan Shamir, founder of Your True Nature and author of *Advice from a Tree*

"Kai's poems (and life!) are a deep bow to the Earth. Words of sweet intimacy with trees, flowers, seeds, and rivers spring from her heart and spirit, drawing us into a deeper communion with the beauty and aliveness all around us."

—Ariana Candell, LMFT, Founder of The Earthbody Institute

Space Between the Stones

Poetry and Practices
for Connecting with
Nature, Spirit, and Creativity

by Kai Siedenburg

Illustrated by Mária Kersey

 Our Nature Connection

Santa Cruz, CA

Copyright © 2020 by Our Nature Connection

ISBN: 978-0-578-67519-0

Cover design by Jeremy Thornton

Cover image by Ian Woolcock

OurNatureConnection.com

SpaceBetweentheStones.com

for all my relations,
and for the benefit of all beings

This book is for you...

yes, you!

This book is for you if...

You have a sense that life could be simpler, saner, and happier.

You long for more authentic and nourishing relationships with yourself and others.

You are drawn to deepen your connection with nature, Spirit, or creativity, and seeking inspiration and support.

You enjoy simple, heartful poetry. (And even if you don't typically enjoy poetry, these poems may speak to you.)

You are awed by the wisdom and wonders of our natural world.

Your heart aches over the state of our planet, and you're seeking encouraging signs amid frightening times.

Despite everything, you have the audacity to hope that a peaceful and thriving world is possible.

And if you're still wondering, please, be my guest— look inside and see if this book really is for you!

Table of Contents

Foreword

Nearly 30 years ago, I was facing a challenging time. I felt stuck. I needed help. One day, I managed to get outside for a neighborhood walk in the fresh Colorado air. I passed a familiar 100-year-old cottonwood tree that I had walked by many times—but this time, something made me stop. Standing at the base of the huge tree, I felt drawn to come closer. As I leaned against the powerful trunk, I felt safe and held. The tree seemed to reach out and wrap its outstretched limbs around me. The connection was made. Timely and beautiful words of wisdom were awakened within me, words that became the poem "Advice from a Tree":

Stand tall and proud
Sink your roots deeply into the Earth
Reflect the light of your true nature
Think long term
Go out on a limb
Drink plenty of water
Remember your roots
Enjoy the view!

Over time, the *Advice from Nature* series grew to include *Advice from a River, Advice from an Owl, Advice from a Sea Turtle, Advice from a Bear* and hundreds more. As the *Advice* continued to spread its hopeful wings, I had the extreme good fortune to meet other kindred spirits of the green and leafy world of nature, including Kai Siedenburg.

When I read her first book, *Poems of Earth and Spirit,* tears often welled up in my eyes. My body trembled with profound recognition that her simple, powerful messages had found a deep and safe place within me. The more I learned about Kai, the more I saw that she was not only writing poetry, but also living poetry and humbly sharing with me and others what she had discovered in her healthy lifestyle of listening to nature, stillness, and service.

I read though the early manuscript of *Space Between the Stones* with great anticipation, and was delighted by what I found. Each poem is better than the next, and resonates with her unique voice and mastery of lightness, surprise, humor, and profound wisdom. I had to force myself to put the book down to save some for later. Like Kai says in her poem, "Rooting":

yes, here,

let's stay
a while,

sink into
the Earth,
and be
nourished.

I am indeed wonderfully nourished by her work, and by her commitment to help us honor and receive the many treasures of nature. In "Seeing the Poems in Everything," Kai describes wanting to find the right words so we can see and feel them too—and she has done it beautifully. Her words breathe life into ink on a page; and her poems and practices offer connection, hope, and useful ideas to help us navigate through each day.

There is much space between these stones, plenty of room to enrich our lives by joining Kai, as she says, in "clearly seeing... the reflection of something much greater." She also writes about viewing herself as a bridge. I completely agree, and the bridge I see is not merely a sterile span of concrete that connects one point to another. It is a finely-crafted expanse over a pristine, flowing river, covered with moss and flowers. Her words invite us to see, feel, hear, taste, and touch the river and who we are more deeply.

Space Between the Stones is written in a language of wonder, a true gift for these changing times and world. I would tell you more, but, my *advice* is: accept the invitation and enter the space Kai has created and meander your own way through...

—Ilan Shamir

Author of *Advice from a Tree, Advice from a River, Words, Tree Celebrations!* and *A Thousand Things Went Right Today!*

Founder of Your True Nature, Inc. and the magical Poetry in Motion Truck

YourTrueNature.com

Facebook.com/PoetryinMotionTruck

Introduction

I'm not exactly sure where these poems come from. I can't pinpoint the location on a map or trace the route via a blue dot on a screen. I do know that when I'm quiet enough inside, I find them in surprising places—not just leaping out from the obvious splendors of a brilliant sunrise or a blooming cherry tree, but also patiently waiting to be discovered in ordinary objects like an old clothesline or new swim goggles. And while I can't command poems to appear, I can create the conditions that make their appearance more likely—just as if you sit still long enough in the forest, birds and other wild creatures may come near.

With few exceptions, these poems come through when I'm alone in a peaceful, natural setting—perhaps lying under a tree and gazing up into the canopy, or sitting on a boulder and watching a stream flow. They arrive when I have enough inner stillness to receive. A few words gently tug at me in a distinctive way that signals their desire to be in a poem. I listen and feel for what wants to come through, writing down the words as they emerge. With practice, I have learned to walk hand in hand with the spirit of the poem, rather than running ahead to where I think it needs to go. When I do this, magic happens. I experience direct communion with something much greater than myself, a powerful sense of being guided with exquisite grace and wisdom. I feel profoundly peaceful, and know that I'm exactly where I need to be.

Writing in this open and receptive way is fairly new for me. For decades, I wrote primarily on assignment for non-profits advocating for just and sustainable food systems. My writing was competent and reliable, but not especially adventuresome or original. It showed up on time and got the job done, but rarely surprised or inspired anyone—including me. If my writing were a person, I might have hired it to do my taxes, but wouldn't have gone on a date or a road trip with it.

During that time, I had a vague inkling that I might have untapped reserves of creativity lying around somewhere, but no clue where to find them. They were like a box of colorful, exotic clothes buried in a storage unit that I had misplaced the key to years ago. This missing key came into my hands quite effortlessly when I took a sabbatical and began spending extended quiet time in nature. It was a time of transition, and I was seeking clarity about my next path of service. I had a strong intuition I would find it by listening to the natural world.

So, instead of going out with friends and talking most of the time, I went out solo and tuned into the sights and sounds of nature. Instead of staying in perpetual motion, I sat still or lay down on the Earth for extended periods of time. I practiced listening deeply to nature, not just with my ears, but with my mind, body, heart, and spirit.

I listened, and the Earth spoke.

I found my new path of service in guiding people into more mindful, intimate, and healing relationships with the natural world. And I discovered a vast wellspring of creation that gave me many unexpected gifts, including hundreds of poems. In just a few months, my lifelong relationship with writing went from pleasant and predictable to profound and passionate.

Most people would say I wrote these poems, and in a narrow sense that is true. Yet I did not write them alone. I co-created them with mountains, trees, birds, and many other generous collaborators in the more-than-human world. I wrote them as part of a beautiful and mysterious flow of creation that became accessible to me through my deep communion with nature. These poems are the fruit of a sacred love triangle between myself, Earth, and Spirit—one in which I am by far the smallest edge, yet essential for conveying them into tangible form.

I think of this as an "Earthly Trinity" of Earth, Spirit and Self, a trio of original bonds that are both profoundly sacred and readily available. When we honor and tend these bonds, we have access to powerful support and abundant reserves of natural intelligence and creativity. We can remember who we are and why we're here.

The poems in this volume speak to the place within each of us that experiences direct communion with Earth and Spirit, or at least senses it is possible. The practices help you to find your own unique paths to deepening these connections. Together, these poems and practices remind you that you are never truly alone, but part of something vast and beautiful. They reveal that simple pathways, walked regularly, will strengthen your core connections and help sustain you no matter what comes.

We live in chaotic and challenging times, with unprecedented threats to the future of life on Earth. We all need ways to stay grounded and nourished, to find glimmers of hope when we are discouraged, to restore our strength when we are weary. Tending our original bonds with Earth and Spirit is one of the best ways we can remain resourced, resilient, and creative in trying times.

May we learn to live in peace and balance with ourselves, each other, and all life on this extraordinary planet!

Seeing Nature, Being Nature

Rooting

It happens
so spontaneously
and effortlessly.

No decision
or deliberate action
is needed.

As soon as I pause
for a few breaths

in the quiet
green forest,

by a clear
flowing stream,

or among
the tall grasses
of the meadow,

I can feel
my roots sprouting,

saying
yes, this,
yes, here…

let's stay
a while,

sink into
the Earth,
and be
nourished.

How the Sky Holds the Sea

Have you noticed
how the sky
holds the sea?

Gently caressing
every inch of her,

letting her know
he's always there,

while allowing her
complete freedom
to move.

Gradual Unfolding

Thank you,
Japanese
maple leaves,

for opening
so gradually…

for giving me
not just
hours or days,
but weeks

to delight
in the miracle
of your unfolding.

A Leaf in the Sun

Today I feel
like a
leaf
in the sun—

thrilled by
the touch
of the light,

grateful
for the gift
of another day,

aware that
all too soon
I will fall.

Who Else but the Leaves?

Who else
but the leaves,

blindsided by
a bitter frost
and facing
certain death,

would summon up
all the unexpressed color
within them

and offer it up
in a final grand gesture
of extravagant beauty?

Becoming Spring

The nights
are still long
and dark,

but each day
there's a little
more light.

The mornings
are still chilly
with frost,

yet the sharp edge
of the cold
is softening.

The branches
are still stark
and bare,

yet their buds swell
with the promise
of vibrant leaves
and bright blossoms.

The bulbs
are still deep
in subterranean
slumber,

yet they are
gently stirring
with dreams
of spring.

The birds,
having flown south
to warmer climes,

are feeling
the familiar tug
to return home.

Yes, it's
still winter,

but it's
becoming spring.

The Great Dance

There are birds
I'll never meet
whose nests
are a bit softer

because I scattered
my hair trimmings
under the lemon tree
instead of confining them
to the trash.

There are plants
I've met just once
who have grown
a little taller and lusher

because I gave
the waters
from my body
to the Earth

instead of
isolating them
in an underground tank,

and other plants
in my garden
I am more intimately
acquainted with—

their bodies
contain even more cells
that were once
part of mine,

as my body
contains cells
that were once
part of theirs.

Meanwhile,
even in distant lands,
trees are
breathing my breath
as I am
breathing theirs.

I am honored
to be a small part
of these great cycles,

thankful
that all the walls
and barriers
of the modern world
can't fully contain me,

that there are still
so many threads
of connection
I can tend
and strengthen.

And when
the day comes
that my spirit leaves
my body,

please don't imprison
my remains
inside a box
or obstruct

the natural progress
of decay
with chemicals.

Let me be free
to return
to the Earth
I came from.

Let my
seemingly
lifeless body
nourish other lives.

Even when I can
no longer move,
I want to continue
being part
of this great dance.

Encounters with Nature

Calling in Well

Please forgive me.

Thank you
for understanding.

Due to
circumstances
far beyond
my control,

I will not
be coming
to work today.

Due to
an extended and
intimate encounter
with the wild splendor
of the Big Sur mountains,

I am still
under the influence
of redwoods
and wildflowers

and unable
to perform
my regular duties.

After multiple
exhilarating plunges
into cold mountain streams,
my animal body
is much too
awake and alive

to tolerate
sitting still
on a chair
in front of a screen
inside a box
for any length of time.

And due to numerous
acts of God,
the Goddess,
and Nature,

I am too
acutely aware
of the profound beauty
and oneness
of all life
to pretend
I am separate,

too aware of the
preciousness
of my own life
to throw it away.

My work here
is done.

I am seeking
a new assignment
more suitable
for my current skills
and experience.

Thank you
for understanding.

In My Skin

In my skin,
I feel…

the light caress
of the breeze,

the warm glow
of the sun,

the cool embrace
of the river

a million
little kisses
that usually
land unnoticed

on the soft shell
of my clothes.

The endless flow
of gentle caresses
calls me home
to this moment,

reminding me
that I am alive,

I am in a body,

and my body
is beautiful.

Barefoot and in Love

Going barefoot,
like falling in love,

leaves tender places
exposed,

makes you vulnerable
to feeling things
you haven't felt
in a long time,
maybe ever,

vulnerable
to feeling things
you didn't
even know
you could—

some deliciously
pleasurable,

some awkward
and uncomfortable,

some downright
terrifying.

And yes,
it carries
the risk
of getting hurt—

but isn't it
worth that risk?

Elemental

It's just
the juncos
and me
out here
today.

Every other animal
seems to be
sensibly sequestered
somewhere warmer,
drier, and safer.

But we
intrepid creatures
are out here
with the howling wind,
driving rain,
and pelting hail.

And we
don't mind
a bit—

truth be told,
we love it!

It quickens
the pulse,

awakens
the senses,

makes us
feel more
fully alive.

It reminds us
that we are part
of something
vast, wild,
and beautiful—

it's elemental.

And later,
when I return
to my cozy cabin,
turn up the heat,

peel off
my rain-soaked clothes
and replace them
with dry ones,

I notice
what a
precious gift it is
simply to be
warm and dry.

Because of
the cold,
I understand warmth
in a new way.

Three Young Skunks

I am certainly
no expert
in skunk parenting,

but I thought
they looked
a little young
to be out
on their own—

three baby skunks,
their bodies
no longer
than my hand,

foraging
in the meadow
at the edge
of the woods,

so fully absorbed
in their task
that they seemed
utterly oblivious
to my presence.

I stepped back
to what I hoped
was a respectful distance—

close enough
to see them,
yet far enough
to avoid triggering fear
in the young skunks

or the wrath
of their mother,
in case she was
standing guard
nearby.

Yet no protective
mother skunk
materialized,
and the babies
remained blissfully
unaware of my presence.

So, we peacefully
coexisted for a while,
the little skunks
contentedly rooting
among the grasses,

me standing
contentedly nearby
and smiling.

On the Road at Night

Driving alone
on a quiet
country road
on a moonless night,

not a single car
or house nearby,

a chorus of crickets
the loudest sound,

the road a
smooth ribbon of black
unspooling seamlessly
into the warm night,

with an occasional
pale curve
punctuating
the blackness
like a question mark.

I stop the car
to investigate,
step out
on to the road,

and encounter
an old friend
I had hoped to see
on the trail that day—

a rattlesnake,
quietly soaking up
the sun's warmth

still lingering
in the now-dark road.

The two of us meet
in silent recognition—
each aware
the other
has the power
to harm

but will wield it
only as a last resort.

Tonight, as usual,
we meet in peace—

just two creatures
breathing together
under the stars,

finding our way home
through the darkness.

A Small Death

Until today,
I had never
cried over
a banana slug.

Until today,
I had never
prayed for one.

Until today,
I had never
stepped on
and killed one.

But today,
it happened.
I was looking up
instead of down
at a fateful moment—

one of those moments
that changes everything.

It almost
surprises me,
the depth of
anguish I feel
over causing the death
of this modest creature.

Compared to all
the suffering
in this world,
it may appear
insignificant.

Yet this loss
is near enough
and small enough
that I can feel it
with my whole heart.

And while
it might seem
inconsequential
to some,
it matters to me—

and it certainly matters
to the banana slug,
and to the unborn
future generations
who will never
come to be,

whose family tree
has lost a branch
because of
one careless
human step.

With a heavy heart
and tears streaming
down my face,
I apologize
yet again,

searching vainly for
an appropriate way
to make amends
for accidentally taking
this humble
yet precious life.

The words of
an ancient Buddhist vow,
buried deep
in the recesses
of my memory,
rise spontaneously to
the surface:

"Sentient beings
are numberless.
I vow to protect them."

And I do!

Winged Mystery

Today, a lovely
yet unfamiliar voice
creates ripples
in the stillness
of the morning.

The elegant,
fluting call,
spiraling gracefully
up and down,

is as near
as the plants
outside my window
and yet
utterly foreign.

I haven't seen
his face,
don't know
his name—

I know nothing
about him
but the sound
of his voice,

yet already he has
stirred my imagination
and captured my heart
with his enchanting song.

Who is he—
this winged man
of mystery?

What does
he look like?

Where did
he come from—

and why now,
after all these years?

There is so much
I want to know.

For now,
I have the beauty
of his song,

and the beauty
of the mystery—

and that
is more than
enough.

Flowing with Water

River Time

When we camp out
at the river,
time flows
differently.

We step out of
the cramped box
of modern life,

which never seems
big enough to hold
everything
we try to cram into it,

and into
a small stretch
of river
that holds
vast expanses
of time—

where hours
are marked
not by
numbers
on a clock,

but by
the ancient rhythms
of day and night,
shadow and light,

flowing effortlessly
like the river.

Into the River

Arriving at the edge
of the river,
I shed
unnecessary layers—

shoes and clothes,
plans and goals,
doubts and woes.

Newly unburdened,
I slip into
the cool green water.

Smooth stones
cradle my bare feet,

flowing water
gently caresses
every inch
of my animal body.

Nothing separates me
from cool water,
warm sun,
the sweetness of birdsong,
the quiet peace of trees.

Nothing separates me
from myself.

Reading the River

There is no need
to bring a book
when I visit
the Yuba River.

An abundant array
of fascinating,
lavishly illustrated
reading material
has already been provided—

granite boulders
sculpted into
sensuous curves,

drifts of smooth,
multi-colored stones,

dragonflies glinting
green and blue in the sun.

Some of the most
illuminating passages
are written
by the intricate,
ever-changing dance
of light and water—

endlessly engaging,
absorbing, and intriguing.

I could read
the river for hours.

And I do!

Flowing with Obstacles

Sitting quietly
by the river,
I notice something
I missed until now:

the constrictions
actually enrich
the flow.

Tumbling over
rocks
and fallen logs,

water makes music,
creates beauty,
breathes in air,
and nourishes
more life.

The apparent obstacles
create safe havens
for myriad creatures

to take refuge,
lay eggs,
and hatch their young.

Ultimately,
the obstacles
make more possible.

Wet, Wild, and Windy

Although
we had
never met,

we exchanged
knowing smiles,

as if to say
"greetings,
fellow adventurer,"

as if to say,
"here we are,
sharing this
extraordinary experience
that most others miss—
aren't we
the lucky ones?"

like members
of a small,
not-so-secret society,

a club
that is open
to many,
yet few
elect to join—

one whose members
willingly walk
along the edge
of the stormy sea
through pouring rain
and howling winds—

who delight in
venturing out
into the wild dance
of the storm,

even if it
sweeps them
off their feet.

Loving the Rain

I'm loving the rain
and the cold and the wet—

I'm loving it more
than I ever have yet.

I love staying inside
and watching it fall,

or going out bundled up—
I'm loving it all.

The soft touch
of droplets
kissing my face,

the smell of moist air,
the fog's gentle embrace.

The joy
of my plant friends
quenching their thirst,

the bright green
of mosses,
the scent
of damp Earth.

Yes, I love
sunny days,
warm skin,
and blue sky,

but no plant or animal
can always be dry.

Natural Wonders

The Songs of Seeds

What if
seeds sang
when they
sprouted?

Imagine
the meadows
ringing
with the
joyous sound

of thousands
of tiny green voices
lifted together
in exultation.

Tiny Yet Mighty

Don't let
their tiny size
and humble appearance
fool you.

Seeds are
heroic voyagers,
venturing forth
into the unknown,

journeying
across time
and space
in search of
friendly soil,

with hidden treasures
sewn into
their modest robes—

the power
to create life,
feed
the hungry,
and transform
a landscape.

Behold
the tiny
yet mighty
seed!

Perpetual Motion

Clouds race by
overhead,
propelled by
a mighty river of air.

Hawks swoop
and soar,
skillfully riding
the swift current.

Trees dance
wildly,
branches tossed
by the gale.

A boundless stream
of sunlight hurtles
through the cosmos
at the speed of light,

and planet Earth
spins through space
at a dizzying rate.

And yet,
at the center
of this vast swirl
of perpetual motion,

there is
an infinite
and abiding
stillness.

Sudden Sunlight

Riding my bike
along a
pleasantly empty road
on a Sunday morning,

feeling quietly contented
to be out
while most others
are still in,

my peaceful mood
is reflected
by a soft, gray blanket
of clouds
and muted
morning light—

until suddenly,
a small opening
appears in the sky.

A patch of blue
is revealed,
an extravagance
of sunlight
pours through,

and my spirit
leaps up
to meet it.

In a heartbeat,
I am transported
from quiet contentment
to spontaneous rapture.

And then,
just as swiftly,
the clouds close,

leaving no trace
of the patch of bright blue
or the sudden sunlight.

But I still feel it
in my body,
and I know
that this light
will shine through me
for the rest
of the day.

Sunshine on a Cloudy Day

Waking today
to a sky of gray
on a day
I'd hoped
for blue,

I briefly entertain
the idle complaint
that there's no sun—

until it dawns on me
that even on this
cold, gray day,

I am bathed
in an extravagance
of light and warmth

generously provided
by our nearest
neighboring star—

more than enough
to keep me comfortable
in a light jacket,

more than enough
to allow me
to clearly see

the vibrant
green leaves
of the oaks,

these words
taking shape
on the blank page,

the path
leading me forward

into a day
that promises
even more abundant
warmth and light.

The Gifts of Stillness

Waking Up Slowly

Slowly

I open

my eyes.

Slowly

I take

my first

waking breaths

of the day.

Slowly
I look around
the room,

noticing sunlight
slanting through
the blinds

and birds singing
just outside
the window.

Slowly
I stretch my arms
up over my head,

noticing
I am in a body
and my body
is breathing.

Slowly
it dawns on me:

although
I have been
unconscious
for hours,
I am still here,
still breathing…

I have
been granted
the extraordinary gift
of another day
to live—

and this day
is precious!

Slowly

I move into
the day,

because life

is too short

to hurry.

The Open Canvas

Today,
there is
no hurry,

no need
to follow
a clock

or meet
a deadline.

Today,
there are
no to-do lists
or marching orders,

no have-to's
or even shoulds,

There is only
the generous,
open canvas
of the day

stretching out
before me,
inviting me
to fill it
with any colors
I choose.

Space Between the Stones

A lesson
I am still learning:

not to toss
stones into the pond
one after the other,

compelled by
a seductive
yet unattainable ideal
of constant
forward motion—

but rather
to allow space
between the stones,

to let
the ripples expand
into stillness

so I can
clearly see
the treasures
just below the surface.

Two Suitors

Two ardent suitors
pursue me
through my days,

displaying
their charms,
vying for my attention,

each convinced
he is the one
for me,

each beseeching me
to take his hand
and let him
guide me across
the dance floor.

One loves to
spin me
around the room
at a dizzying pace,

compelled by
the driving tempo
that is
all the rage
these days.

The other
holds me close,
moving slowly,
whispering in my ear,

"there's no hurry…
you are free to follow
your own rhythms,
no matter how slow,
no matter
what everyone else
is doing."

Which one
will win
my hand today?

Which one
will I invite
to guide me
across the floor?

What I Slow Down For

I slow down for flowers
I slow down for trees

I slow down to notice
the birds and the bees.

I slow down for beauty
I slow down for grace

I slow down for
the kiss of the sun
on my face.

I slow down to meditate
I slow down to pray

I slow down at the beginning
and end of the day.

I slow down for my body,
my nerves, and my heart.

I slow down for music.
I slow down for art.

I slow down when it matters
I slow down when I care

I slow down for clean water,
fertile soil, and fresh air.

I slow down to notice
I slow down to feel

I slow down to relax,
replenish, and heal.

I slow down to listen
I slow down to see

I slow down to remember
I slow down just to be.

God Does Not Like to Hurry

God
does not like
to hurry.

The Beloved
doesn't want
to be compressed
into a few
cramped moments

before you bolt down
your breakfast
and rush out the door,

or a half-hearted,
mumbled prayer
as you collapse into bed
after another
exhausting day.

God wants
to meet you
in wide open spaces
and relaxed expanses
of time—

to sit quietly with you
on a mountaintop,
beholding the miracle
of the sunrise,

to dance with you
in a meadow
under a starry sky,

to flow freely
through you
and all around you
as you rest into
a generous span
of stillness.

Yes, God can
squeeze into
the smallest slivers of time
in a day of non-stop activity—

But why settle
for a thimbleful
of the Divine

when you could have
a vast ocean?

*Poet's note: In most cases, I use the word "Spirit"
rather than "God," because I see it as more inclusive.
However, this poem clearly wanted to say "God," so I
honored its request. If that word doesn't resonate for
you, I invite you to substitute one that does—Spirit,
the Divine, the Beloved, and the Universe are a few
good options.*

In the Stillness

In the stillness,
I find...

refuge from
the relentless demands
and distractions
of modern life,

a chance
to step off
the treadmill,
shed unnecessary layers,

and slip into
a deeper, truer
current,

space for
my spirit
to unfurl her
magnificent wings

and soar above
the mundane details
of daily life,

so many treasures
that fell
by the wayside

as I was
hurrying along,
trying in vain
to keep up.

In the stillness,
a calm pool
where I can
clearly see
my own reflection,

and the reflection
of something
much greater
than myself.

Simply Being

Right now,
simply being here,

savoring this stillness,
is more important than

washing dishes,

planting kale,

tasting ripe figs
at the farmers' market,

or a hundred other
pleasurable
or productive
things I could do.

Right now,
simply holding still
and being

is the best way
I know

to cherish
the precious gift
of this morning.

The Right to Remain Silent

You have the right
to remain silent.

In a world
crowded with sounds
and buzzing with
electronic signals,

as endless waves
of ringtones and alerts
wash over you,

and especially
when everyone else
is clamoring
to be heard—

you have the right
to remain silent.

—

You have the right
to remain still.

Amidst
the seemingly
ceaseless swirl
of the modern world,

while an
alarmingly over-developed
to-do list
shouts at you
from your desk,

and especially when
everyone else
is hurrying
through ostensibly urgent
yet often unimportant tasks—

you have the right
to remain still.

———

You have the right
to remain calm.

In the midst of
a flood
of virtual signals
designed to incite
artificial urgency,

in the face of
a tsunami
of terrifying news
about the state
of our planet,

and especially when
everyone else
seems consumed
with worry
about what our future
may hold—

you have the right
to remain calm.

———

Faced with so many
compelling reasons
to be anxious,
overwhelmed,
and hurried—

indeed,
precisely because
there are
so many reasons
we could be
anxious,
overwhelmed,
and hurried—

we have the right
to remain
silent,
still,
and calm,

to find a
peaceful place
at the center
of the storm
where we can go
to be restored,

so that we can
return to the fray
with renewed strength,

as a beacon
of peace and presence,
lighting the path
to another way
of being.

Everyday Spirituality

Dancing with Spirit

Now and then,

I gaze up
from the
dense thicket
of daily work
and concerns

long enough
to notice

that I am
not just
toiling away alone
at an endless
series of tasks,

but actually
gliding across
a sacred dance floor,

cradled
in the loving arms
of Spirit.

Invisible

All morning
the Spirit
has been
speaking
to me,

and I've
been listening.

All morning
I have honored
    slower ways of moving...
    quiet ways of listening...
    subtle ways of acting

like roots
moving unseen
beneath the surface,

carrying on
the invisible
yet essential work

that makes
all visible growth
possible.

Not Knowing

I am willing
to not know—

to linger
in that shadowy,
in-between place,

in the
sometimes
awkward silence.

I am willing
to hold
the part of me
that is afraid
of the dark—

that desperately
wants to run
headlong
toward the first
faint glimmer
of light,
no matter the source.

I am willing
to have the patience
to wait
until the mud settles
and my mind
is clear,

to trust
the fertility
of stillness,

to seek
the clearer, brighter light
that burns
just beyond
the dark shadows.

Every Moment

Every moment
the grasses
grow a little taller,

the buds
a bit closer
to being blossoms.

Every moment
clouds drift and shift
into new ways of being,

more of the fallen oak
finds new life as soil,

and countless creatures
breathe their first breath

while others
take their last.

Every moment
a fleeting moment,
falling
even as it arises,

like a drop of water
flowing swiftly
toward the sea.

Step into the water.

Taste it
while you
still can.

Seeing the Dust

It's mostly
little bits of us,
they say,

floating through the air,
coming to rest
on any available surface,

and, given enough time,
covering it with a
soft, gray blanket.

Mostly
we see it
as a mundane
fact of life
or a minor annoyance—

the endless accumulation
of tiny particles
of our skin
on every nearly-level surface.

Yet it is also
a subtle reminder
that we are not
entirely solid,

but rather
ever-changing,
with 50 billion or so
of our own cells
dying and being replaced
every day.

We are literally
not the same people
we were yesterday,
or who we'll be
tomorrow.

Even as we live
and breathe,
feeling
more or less solid
and distinctly ourselves,

we are gradually
dissolving,
releasing
the boundaries of
our individual forms

into the
formless
and infinite.

Natural Meditation

Whenever I visit
my favorite
Buddhist retreat center,

auspiciously positioned
on a sunny, oak-studded ridge
with panoramic views
of lushly wooded slopes,

I silently give thanks
that I am not
among the ranks
of diligent,
disciplined
meditators

who are spending
most of the day
sitting on their cushions
inside their cabins

while outdoors
thousands of
tiny brown seeds
sprout into
lush green life,

tightly furled buds
come one day closer
to flowering,

diaphanous creatures
spread their wings
and take their first flight,

and all manner
of everyday miracles
unfold.

I admire
the meditators'
dedication.

I salute
their discipline.

I honor the virtues
of their practice,

and I'm grateful
for its profound gifts.

Yet I'm also grateful
that I am not
bound by it.

I give thanks
that my core practice
not only allows me
to be out
under the open sky,
among the trees
and flowers,
but actually
requires it.

I give thanks
that I find deep peace
and transcendence
in meditating on
the wonders
of the natural world.

The Nature of Creation

Seeing the Poems in Everything

Sometimes
I wish
I had magical
poetry vision

that would
allow me
to see
the poems
in everything,

and then find
just the right words
so that you
could see
and feel them too.

Sometimes,
for fleeting
and precious
moments,
I do.

Stumbling Toward Poetry

Lines of poems
stumble about,

struggling to
arrange themselves
into coherent
and graceful forms,

their steps
halting and clumsy,
like dancers
with two left feet.

It has been so long
since they tried
to move
like this.

Still,
I can see
the beauty
in their yearning,

the grace
just beyond
their awkwardness.

When I Meet a Poem

When I sense
a poem approaching,

I put aside
whatever
I am doing
and prepare
to meet it,

seeking to
make of myself
a clear
and open path,

a willing
and worthy vessel,

a humble
and faithful servant

of something
much greater
than myself—

"not my will,
but thine."

Sharing the Treasure

Yes,
part of me
longs
to turn my back
on this crazy world,

walk deep
into the forest,

and never return.

Yet even more
than that,

I want to
walk deep
into the forest

and return
to share the
treasures
I receive there.

Creation Coming

I can sense
creation coming—

in the
deepening stillness,

the clear call
to be quiet
and listen,

in soft stirrings
I can sense
but not yet see—

like a magnificent,
winged being

approaching
through the
twilight woods,

moving silently
over dry leaves,

inviting me to ride
on her powerful back
to beautiful
and mysterious realms.

I am ready.

Trusting in Creation

Sometimes
trusting in creation
means
simply sitting still
as sacred gifts
flow into
my open palms—

and sometimes
it means
waiting patiently
for hours,
holding
my empty bowl,

having faith
that eventually
something
will come.

Sometimes
it means
filling my vessel
with clear water
from a
free flowing spring—

and sometimes
trudging for miles
under the blazing sun
in search for
a faint trickle
of muddy water.

Sometimes
it means
walking a rocky path
on a moonless night—

and sometimes
saying yes
to a bright
and brilliant light.

Painting by the Numbers

As a young girl,
I adored
paint-by-the-numbers kits,

and spent
many happy hours
following
their formulas,

meticulously
applying color
between the lines

to replicate
the image of kittens
or horses
on the box cover.

I found safe haven in
the clear parameters
and predictable outcomes,

willingly relinquished
artistic freedom
to a benevolent dictatorship

that would never lead
to originality or beauty,

but did offer
a sense of security
to a child
hungry for
order and predictability.

Now that little girl
is more or less
grown up,

and no longer
clings so tightly
to illusions
of assured outcomes.

Now, she paints
with words,

and has learned
to embrace
the mystery
of creation,

to love the freedom
of a blank page

that invites her
to write
whatever
her heart desires.

The Artist's Path

The Artist in Her Cage

Sometimes
I leave my artist
in a cage

while I go off
to do the things
responsible adults
are supposed to do.

As far as
cages go,
it's not bad—

it has a few
potted plants,
access to sunlight
and shade,

and plenty
of food
and water.

For a while,
she is alert,
active,
even playful,

taking interest
in her surroundings,
watching for
my return,

anticipating
the moment
of her release.

Yet if
I stay away
too long,

the light
in her eyes
grows dim
and she becomes
listless,

spending
her days
lying in a corner
of the cage

while the dream
of the wildness
she was born for
silently
slips away.

The Artist Takes a Stand

Once again,
the artist
has appeared
on my threshold

in the middle
of the night,
pounding urgently
on the door,

seeking refuge
from a horde
of cruel taskmasters
who are
in hot pursuit,
torches blazing,

threatening
to burn her sanctuary,
carry her off,

and conscript her
into their massive army
of wage slaves.

She knows
how ruthless
they can be.

She fears
for her creative life.

Yet all
is not lost.

She will not
be saved
by a handsome prince
or an army
of brave warriors.

She will not
be saved
by fighting
fire with fire—

nor by fleeing
from the fire.

She will be saved
by retreating
into her sanctuary,
pulling up
the drawbridge,

and standing quietly
in her own power—

and in a power
much greater
than her own.

The Artist on Strike

My artist
is on strike,
demanding
fair working conditions
and a living wage.

Truth be told,
she doesn't actually
want to strike—

she would much rather
do the creative work
that she is here to do.

Yet sometimes
the pressures
become so unreasonable,
the conditions
so intolerable,

that she has
little choice
but to lay down
her pen
and stand up
for her rights—

protection from
cruel taskmasters
and harsh critics,

regular access
to beauty
and inspiration,

and enough
time, space,
and freedom
to follow creative ideas
wherever they may
lead her.

Is that
too much
to ask...

for her?

for any of us?

The Artist's Path

My artist
walks her own path.

She does not
follow the prescribed course,
color inside the lines,
or sit quietly
waiting to be called on.

She does not always do
what is expected,
or do it the way
it's always been done.

She is not hiding
safely in the middle
of the bell curve
or near the center
of the herd.

She does not
always fit in.

She is marching
(no, not marching—
she is dancing!)
to the beat
of a different drummer,

singing her own song,
making her path
by walking it.

She is following
the light of a distant star,

one that calls her forward
even when the path
is steep and rocky,

even when
it's so dark that
she can't see
the next step
or if she's still
on the path.

Not because
she wants
to be different.

Not because
she wants
to be special.

Not because
she wants attention.

But because
of what she knows
is true,
even when
she can't see it
or put her finger on it,

Because the light
of that distant star
shines so clearly
and brightly,

Because her very life
depends on it.

The Artist Takes the Reins

Perhaps
this is why
those charged with
maintaining order

so rarely
hand over the reins
to the artist.

Once again,
she has
turned the steed
away from
the established path

and is galloping
headlong
toward freedom,

eyes flashing,
long hair flying.

The Free-Range Artist

Believe it or not,
my artist
is a lot like
a chicken.

If you cram
her into a tiny cage
inside a big factory
and pressure her
to work
365 days a year,

she will still produce,
but her life will be
"nasty, brutish,
and short,"

and you will taste it
in every egg.

If, on the other hand,
you give her
plenty of fresh air,
green pasture,
and room to roam,

you will taste
freedom and joy
in every egg.

Her body
will know
the difference,
and so will yours.

Feeding My Artist

My artist
follows a
special diet.

She does not
respond well to
the standard fare

of overwork,
screen time,
and suppressing
natural longings.

Like the mammal
she is,
she loves
to be outside
under the open sky,
among the trees
and birds,

to roam freely,
attune to the beauty
and wisdom of nature,

and listen
for what
wants to come.

Like many
untamed creatures,
she thrives on
quiet,
solitude, and
freedom—

freedom to wander,
to notice what calls her,
to follow her own path,
to trust her own voice.

The Muse Asked Me to Remind You...

The muse asked me
to remind you
that although she is
a vast, powerful being
with infinite reserves
of creativity,

she is also
like a child
who requires
regular care
and attention
to thrive.

She asked me
to remind you
that although
her needs are simple
and she can endure
many challenges
and setbacks,

you will need
to feed her
to keep her alive—

and that she will
languish on a diet
of pressure and busyness,

and flourish
on a diet
of freedom
and kindness.

She asked me
to remind you
that although
she can tolerate
some neglect

and regular,
even daily
questioning
of her gifts,

that as much
as she wants
to stay
by your side,

even in the face of
the sad parade of
doubts and distractions
that pull you away from
her loving embrace,

she, too,
has her limits—

and if you put her
in a dark closet,

forget about her,

and don't come back
until years later,

she may
not
be there.

The Lighter Side

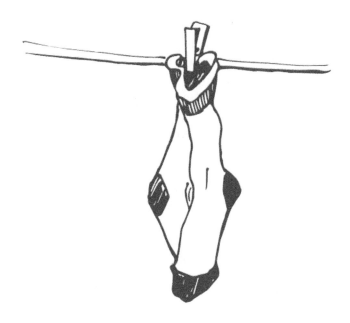

Not to Fear

So many things
we're taught to fear
needn't be so frightful—
I'll name some here.

Things that slither
Things that scurry
Things with scales
Things that are furry

Things with six legs
Things with eight
Things that boldly leap
Things that hesitate

Things bigger than a breadbox
or smaller than a hair

Things swimming in the water
or flying through the air

Things that go bump
or howl in the night

Things that screech or yowl
in broad daylight

Even those
with fangs and claws
so rarely mean us harm.

They're just
trying to get by—
there's no cause for alarm.

Some things in life
are truly scary—

but most of those
aren't scaly or hairy.

The Formidable Fly

Rattlesnakes?
Hardly seen or heard.

Mountain lions?
A rare and
distant danger.

Right now,
the most
formidable creature
in the forest,

the only one
with the power
to command
most of my attention
and cut short
my long-anticipated hike,

is not
a venomous viper
or a ferocious feline,

but rather
the lowly fly
who, despite
its diminutive size
and utter lack
of fangs, claws,
or other overt weaponry,

and armed with nothing
but a single-minded focus
on relentlessly flinging itself
against my eyes and nose,

driven by
an obsessive quest
for the holy grail
of a bit of moisture,

is the only creature
with the power
to drive me
to distraction
and send me
fleeing
for the safety
of my little cabin.

I withstand the test,
but just barely.

An Unexpected Gift

Setting out
for a solo hike
on a rainy day,

I slip my keys
into a pocket
of my pack

and touch something
my fingers
are surprised
to encounter—

a small package
of chocolate almonds.

My heart leaps
to an almost
embarrassing height.

But why not?

The start of
a rainy hike
is a perfect moment
to discover this
unexpected pleasure,

like an
encouraging message
sent and then
promptly forgotten
by an earlier
version of myself,

or a surprise gift
from an eccentric
yet loveable aunt

who I am
increasingly
coming to resemble.

The Perfectionist Catches a
Glimpse of Herself

Even though
it's dark,

even though
she is at
a remote
Buddhist retreat center,

even though
the few other people there
are all safely sequestered
in the meditation hall

and no one
will see her,
much less care—

despite all this,
before she steps out of
the bathhouse,
she takes a moment
to locate
the subtle seam
in her blue fleece hat

(barely detectable
even at close range
and under bright light)

and turns it
so it's at the back
of her head,
as she has done
hundreds of times—

whether or not
anyone was there
to notice.

At least
this time
she catches herself
and laughs.

As Is

One human,
as is.

Original owner.

Approximately
350,000 miles.

Very reliable
if regular
maintenance
is performed.

All parts
in working order,

but some
minor defects
and visible
signs of wear.

Guaranteed
to last
a lifetime,

which can be
greatly extended
through
diligent maintenance.

Just Out of Reach

Have you ever
searched for
a familiar word,

only to discover
that it was
just beyond
your grasp,

like an oft-used object
on a high shelf
that you once
reached with ease—

something you know
is still there,
right where
you left it

and yet now
maddeningly
out of reach,

just a few
millimeters beyond
where your
once-limber memory
can stretch?

The Old Clothesline Takes a Stand

For months now,
I've been expecting
the old clothesline
to break.

To my eyes,
the thinning bundle
of fibers
doesn't look
nearly strong enough

to support
the weight
of wet towels and sheets
captivated by
the powerful allure
of gravity.

And yet,
somehow,
it is.

Somehow,
those aging
and apparently frail fibers,
pulling together,
are strong enough
to bear a heavy load,

strong enough
to accomplish
so much more
than I expect
of them.

For months now,
a new clothesline
has been standing by,
sleek and shiny,
bursting with
youthful vigor
and enthusiasm,

eager to
step into its vocation
and fulfill its date
with destiny.

But the
old clothesline says
"not so fast—
I'm not dead yet!"

Oy, Sky!

"Here,"
the sky said,
"have some more,"

as she piled my plate high
with extra helpings
of gray clouds and rain.

I gave her
a look.

"What?!"
she exclaimed,
"you don't like
my cooking?!"

"Oh no,"
I replied,
"it's delicious,"
patting my belly
to underscore
the point—

"it's just that
I'm so full."

"Nonsense!"
she cried,
"you're too skinny!"

as she heaped
yet another
enormous scoop
of clouds and rain
on my already-full plate.

I smiled weakly,
lifted my fork,
and attempted to
clear my plate
yet again—

I didn't want
to be rude.

For days
it went on
like this,

until finally
I could take
no more.

"Oy, sky,"
I said,
"enough already!"

I put down
my fork,
pushed back
from the table
and stepped outside.

The clouds parted,
and a brilliant shaft
of sunlight
illuminated
my empty plate.

Starting to Stop

I am starting
to stop,

doing
more less,

catching up
with slowing down.

I am shifting quickly
into the slow lane,

being deliciously
inefficient,

doing the "nothing"
that is really
something!

Today I
torpedoed
my to-do list,

sent my taskmaster
packing
for a mandatory
vacation,

let my inner child
out to play

and my inner puppy
off her leash.

I did nothing
on a list
and everything
in my heart,

nothing with
a deadline
and everything
with lifeline.

I said no
with a
bigger yes
in mind.

Getting Personal

Never Too Late

On the outside,
an independent
woman,

walking
with a
confident stride,

moving
through the world,

doing
what needs
to be done.

On the inside,
a little girl—

tired of
playing dress-up
in the grown-up suit

that was always
too big
for her young
shoulders,

longing to
slip into
the soft,
little-girl dress—

the one
with
the butterflies,

the one
that fits her
small body
perfectly,

the one
she always
dreamed of,

even while
it remained
hidden
at the back
of the closet—

so far back
that everyone
forgot
it was there.

Is it true
what they say?

Is it true
it's never
too late

to have
a happy childhood?

Kitty Dreams

Her lithe, supple body
lies draped over my legs,
completely at rest,

every muscle and sinew
slack and still
except for
the gentle
rise and fall
of her breath.

For many moments
we remain
like this,

breathing
each other's breath,

no other movement
rippling the stillness,

her small life
humming
so close to mine.

And then her legs
begin twitching gently,
her face too,
and low moans
escape her mouth.

I smile and wonder
where her dreams
have carried her.

Is she roaming
through a meadow,
stalking some small prey,

or climbing a tree
to escape
a real
or imagined threat?

As I sense
each subtle movement
of her body,

I marvel
at this intimacy
with a once-wild creature

that she feels
safe enough
to share my bed,

to surrender to sleep
while sprawled
across my body,

to allow me
to feel her dreams,

to trust me
with her life.

Alone, Yet Not Lonely

When you see me
hiking by myself

sitting at the river
by myself

eating lunch
by myself

do you see
isolation and
loneliness?

do you
pity my sad plight
as a woman alone?

Or can you sense
what I actually feel—

profound peace
and contentment,

a solid core
of inner strength,

delicious freedom
to follow
my own rhythms?

Can you sense
that I am
anything but lonely,
indeed not even
really alone—

that I have at last
abandoned
the perennial quest
for one true love

and come home
to the love
within me
and all around me?

Unspoken

So much
remains
unspoken.

So much
lingers
in the vast,
uncharted shadows
between the words,

like a kingdom
of small forest creatures
that emerge
only at night—

at home
in the shadows,
yet longing
for the light.

River of Tears

Once again,
a great storm
has moved
through me—

a river of tears
so mighty,
I feared
it might
carry me away.

Yet I have
not been washed
out to sea
or dashed
against the rocks.

I have not
drowned
in a river
of my own tears.

I am still here—
both feet
firmly planted
on the shore.

I am still here—
rain-soaked and
storm-tossed,

yet also cleansed
and unburdened.

Much has been
washed away,

yet my
essential core
remains—

cleaner,
clearer,
shining brightly
in the sun.

Mine of Sadness

This mine
of sadness
has been here
as long
as I can remember,

and indeed
long before that.

Each time
some new wound
plunges me down
into that dark shaft,

I feel both
the weight
of my fresh pain

and the residues
of ancient pain
left by
long-gone ancestors—

pulling me downward,
away from
the brightness above,

telling me
that this is how
it will always be,

that I will never
find my way out again.

Yet no matter
how far
I descend
into the darkness,
I always find my way back,

and each time
I carry
a brighter light
and return with
more gold.

Walking into the Water

There are
so many ways
to walk
into the water.

Some of us
venture in
just a few inches,
pant cuffs rolled up,
to stroll along
the edge
of the ocean,

or to stand
a friendly vigil as
our young children
splash and play.

Some of us
walk farther
into the water
and find ourselves
at home for a time,

our bodies suspended
between sea and sky,
stroking smoothly
through the liquid blue.

Some of us
stride confidently
into the waves
carrying a surfboard,

and stride back out
hours later
feeling exhilarated
and more fully alive.

And some of us
walk into the water
weighed down by
a heavy burden
of grief—

and never
walk out
again.

After the Hospital

After I leave
the hospital
where my only mother
now lies,
recovering from
an unexpected
and frightening surgery,

clear plastic tubes
carrying the fluids
her body
is not yet able
to manage on its own,

a line of
17 metal stints
and a thick white dressing
protecting the site
of the invasion—

that tender place
in her belly
where cells
had been multiplying
with reckless abandon,
unseen and unknown...

After I leave behind
the maze of tubes,
beeping machines,
and bustling nurses,

I step through
heavy glass doors
into what now feels

like a strange
and foreign realm,

where I am astonished
to discover
the sun shining brightly
in a boundless blue sky,

and life going on
as though nothing
has changed.

(Don't they know?!)

And later,
walking by the ocean
on that sunny Saturday,
I feel like a visitor
from a dark and distant land,

stunned and bewildered
by scenes of
everyday beauty
and ordinary joy—

sunlight sparkling
on the water,

couples holding hands
as they stroll
down the beach,

children laughing
and shouting
at the edge
of the waves—

as though
everything is fine...

as though we are
actually safe
inside these
fragile bodies...

as though we
and our dearest beloveds
can count on
being here
tomorrow

and the next day

and the next.

Our Modern World

The Fire of Convenience

We gather
around the fire
as humans have done
for millions of years—
yet how
times have changed.

None of us had to
gather wood and kindling,
drill with a stick
to spark the first flame,
or even strike
a single match.

We simply
turned a dial,
and flames
magically leapt up
over the remarkably realistic
faux logs,
like an obedient genie
responding to our command.

Our bellies are full of food
that other people
grew, harvested,
packaged, and shipped
to the nearby supermarket.

We simply pushed a cart
down the aisles,
gathering a vast bounty
in a matter of minutes,
and slid a plastic card
to make it ours.

We lounge comfortably
in clothing
made by people
on the other side
of the world—

far more cheaply
and easily
than we could have
made it ourselves.

As humans have
always done,
we share stories
around the fire.

Yet they are no longer
our own stories
of what we saw on the land
or made with our hands,

nor are they
ancient wisdom
wrapped in humor
and worn smooth
by centuries of telling.

Instead, we trade in
the modern currency
of stories from
"reality TV" shows

about people
surviving "alone"
in the wilderness,

far removed
from other humans
and the comforts
of civilization,

building shelters,
hunting and foraging
for food,
fashioning clothes
from plant fibers
and animal skins.

(Can you imagine?)

Such a life
is thrilling
to contemplate
from this
safe distance.

It calls to
a part of us
that yearns
to know
and be known
by the wild,

to gather
our own food
and nesting materials,

to see
a blazing canopy of stars
and hear
the songs of coyotes.

Yet all of us
will choose
to remain here,

in the land
of modern conveniences,
close to the refrigerator
and the 24-hour supermarket,

where it seems
that anything we want
can be summoned
with a few taps
on a screen
or a quick car trip,

and yet so much
of what really matters
is being lost.

The Traveling Swim Goggles

The swim goggles
I ordered
arrived on my doorstep
today—

packaged in a box
much larger
than necessary,

swathed in more
plastic packing material
than necessary,

weary after a journey
of hundreds of miles
from a "fulfillment center"

and thousands
of miles
from their birthplace
in China.

The joy
I might otherwise feel
about their arrival

is eclipsed
by sadness
and shame.

This is not
how I want
to do it.

Given a choice,
I would
ride my bike two miles
to Jerry's Sports

and buy my goggles
from the kind couple
who have been part
of our community
for decades,

raising their kids,
supporting soccer teams
and other local businesses.

Given a choice,
I would opt for
a transaction including
a friendly,
face-to face exchange

peppered with
helpful tips
on how to make
my swimsuit last longer
and which earplugs
are best.

But increasingly
I am not offered
that choice.

Like so many other
local businesses,
Jerry's Sports
closed their doors for good
years ago.

There is no longer
a nearby store
where I can buy
swim goggles or
camera batteries,

find a decent selection
of towels or bedsheets,

or have my shoes
or CD player
repaired.

Where is it
all leading,

this brave new world
of nearly instantaneous delivery
of millions of items
from far away?

Two Amazons

The Amazon
is burning.

Trees, plants, animals,
trillions of living treasures
consumed by the blaze,

the "lungs of the Earth"
filled with smoke,

the homes of
countless creatures
destroyed.

Such massive devastation
of intelligent life
is too painful to watch,
more than
our hearts can bear.

Meanwhile,
a very different Amazon
vies for our attention,

luring us
with millions of products,
one-click ordering,
free two-day shipping—

a convenient,
compelling distraction,
as close
as the nearest screen,
(usually closer
than the nearest person),

selling the illusion
of easy, painless
consumption,
the full price tag hidden
behind a shiny curtain.

Which of these
two Amazons
will receive
our precious attention
and money?

Which one
will we keep alive
as the Earth burns?

I Wish I Had an Elder

I wish I had an elder
who could teach me
which acorns
are best to eat
and when to gather them,

and how to make a fire
using only my hands
and what I can find
in the woods.

I wish I had an elder
who could teach me
about where
the chickadees nest
and what kind of hawk
this feather came from,

and the songs
people have sung
for thousands of years
to welcome the rain
or give thanks for the hunt.

I wish I had an elder
who could
help me understand
my dream about
climbing a steep
and narrow trail,

and what it means
to be a leader
at this time.

True, that elder
probably wouldn't
give me
a simple, direct answer.

They would tell a story
that would take a while
to get there,

and that might not
ever arrive at
an answer
that I could discern—

yet it would be
a rich and beautiful journey,
one that held answers
to more questions
than I knew
how to ask.

But who has time
for those stories now?

We're busy people,
and we need information
right away.

Now, we have Google,
which can search
millions of sites
in a fraction of a second,
and mostly deliver
just the information
we ask for.

But Google can't
see beyond
what I type
or browse,

can't look
into my eyes
or my heart,

can't sit with me
while I weep,
or tell me
about the time
it felt
just like I do.

Google didn't know
my mother as a baby,
or the stories of
my ancestors—

all the things
they did
that made it possible
for me to be here today,

Google doesn't know
how to tell me a story
that is big enough
to hold my people
and the land
that sustains us

and small enough
to help me
find my place
in it.

Poemlets

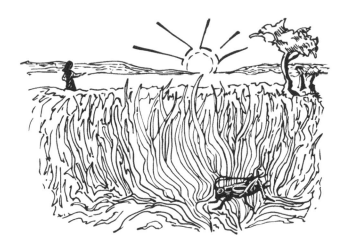

In the morning
in the meadow
with the rising sun

a woman
and a cricket

each singing
her song.

———

Thank you,
birds,

for reminding me
that every sunrise

is cause
for celebration.

———

Sunrise
is a miracle
that happens
every day.

———

Just beyond
the dark clouds,

a brilliant
ball of light.

With flowers,
as with people,

I sometimes
forget a name,

but rarely
forget a face.

—

Sitting
with the creek,
I remember
how to flow.

—

It's so quiet,
I can hear
the trees
growing.

—

First rain
in the mountains.

The trees and I
lift our branches,

opening to receive
the goodness.

The more
I dissolve
into the forest,

the more
I discover
my true form.

—

As a parent
of numerous poems,

my task
is not
to write
the words
for them,

but to
help them find
their own words.

—

Sometimes
the best way
to keep going

is to stop.

Come, mind,
let us sit
quietly
together.

I will
hold you
so you
can rest.

—

When I
hold still
enough,

when I
listen deeply
enough,

gifts fall into
my open hands
like ripe plums.

—

Some prayers
require no words.

They flow directly
from our hearts
to the Divine

like rivers
flowing
to the ocean.

Sometimes
even a prayer
seems like
too many words.

God can
hear me
clearly
in the silence.

—

Aware that
each day
is a gift,

available
for a
limited time only,

I attempt
to conduct myself
accordingly.

—

Can you hear it?

Can you feel it?

The Universe
quietly
cheering
you on?

Practices for Deepening Connection

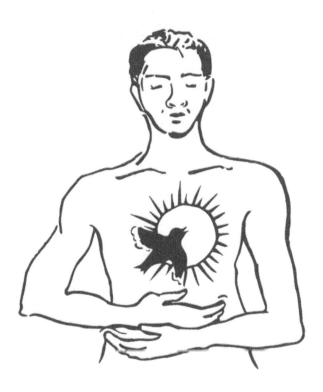

Dear Reader,

Welcome to the practices chapter of *Space Between the Stones!* I hope the poems in this volume have brought you solace and delight, and inspired you to cultivate deeper connections of your own. For at its heart, this book is an invitation into nourishing connections—with nature and Spirit, yourself and loved ones, and authenticity and creativity.

We all need connection to know we're not alone, to understand ourselves and others, to ease our burdens and amplify our joys. And not merely fleeting, superficial exchanges, but deep, authentic ones that feed our spirits and give our lives meaning. Ultimately, the quality of our connections determines the quality of our lives.

However, our modern society creates enormous obstacles to deeper connection, including chronic overwork and long commutes, information overload, social isolation, and limited access to nature. Most of us spend more time looking at screens than into another's eyes, more time sitting indoors than walking on the Earth, and more time working than playing with our friends—both human and more-than human.

Our devices lure us with a shiny promise of easy and constant connection, yet too often pull us away from the present moment and the people and places around us. Still, true connection can be surprisingly simple to attain. It may be as near as our breath, the person in the next cubicle, or the oak tree outside our window.

The practices in this chapter are designed to make authentic connection easy, enjoyable, and rewarding. They are written for busy people, and many can be done in as little as a minute or two. If you have more space in your life, you can give them more time and go deeper. Most work well in a range of settings, and can be done on your own, with one other person, or in a group.

It may help to think of them as a menu of options. You don't have to "order" them all at once—or ever. Notice which ones entice you, try one or two at a time, and see if you feel called to continue those practices or to sample others.

These practices focus on three of the most primal and nourishing bonds available to us as humans: our connections with nature, Spirit, and creativity. Tending these core bonds connects us with our true selves and with something greater than ourselves. It brings us strength and support, helps us be healthy and whole, and allows us to access and express our unique gifts.

These three bonds were woven into the fabric of daily life of virtually every culture on Earth—until our Western culture took hold, with its notions that we are separate from nature, that Spirit is disembodied, and that creativity is the province of a privileged few. Today's fast-paced and techno-centric culture further amplifies the sense of disconnection, teaching us that these core bonds are available only under certain conditions, or luxuries of time we can't afford.

Yet all three of these bonds are more present in our daily lives and more readily accessible than we realize—like a lovely park with a partially hidden entrance that we could easily walk through but haven't yet noticed. They are also thoroughly intertwined, like tree roots growing together and sharing nutrients, so tending any one of them can strengthen all of them. Deepening our connection with nature offers a direct and scenic path to communion with Spirit and creative inspiration. Connecting with Spirit can enhance our reverence for nature and give rise to original creation. Honoring and expressing creativity can enrich our bonds with both nature and Spirit.

The three sets of practices are rooted in a few common elements that make deeper connection possible: slowing down, being present, allowing space, being open and receptive, and giving thanks.

Each time we choose a moment of deeper connection, we create a small oasis of calm and stillness. The more we do this, the more numerous and expansive these oases become, and the easier they are to access. These moments ripple out and soon it seems that people are kinder, good things come our way, and life isn't such a struggle.

May the following practices help you discover your own oases of calm and stillness, and may the benefits ripple out far and wide!

Tips for Using These Practices

Identify your why. What is your intention in doing these practices? What do you hope to gain? Reflecting on this will motivate you and guide you to practices that work for you. Journaling, sharing with a loved one, or walking or sitting quietly in nature can help you to find your why.

Give yourself permission. Many of us are overwhelmed and feel like we don't have time to slow down or take care of ourselves. Write yourself a permission slip that names why it's important for you to do a practice, how it will benefit you and those around you, and what you're giving yourself permission to do. Sign it and read it aloud when you're done.

Notice which practices you feel called to do and give yourself plenty of space to explore and try new things, including those that seem silly, that scare you, or that you think you can't do.

Start small. Starting small is much better than not starting at all, or overreaching and getting discouraged. A little can go a long way. Perhaps your goal is to practice yoga or walk in nature an hour a day, but what's doable right now is five minutes a day or an hour once a week.

Find the time and space that work for you. Integrating practices with daily activities makes them more doable and reminds you to do them. And regular practice, even just a minute a day, is powerful—it builds the connection, amplifies the benefits, and motivates you to continue. You might want to meditate before breakfast, go for a mindful walk at lunch, or write in a gratitude journal at bedtime. Consider doing a brief practice every day and a longer one at least once a week (and if possible, occasional daylong or overnight retreats to deepen your practice).

Creating physical space for a practice also is powerful. This may be as small as a special journal for writing or a modest altar for meditation, or as large as a studio dedicated to your art.

Unplug. Taking breaks from electronic devices reduces stress and anxiety and helps you be more present and available to connect. Unhook the electronic leash by turning off your phone, putting it in a separate room, or leaving it behind. (The farther it is from your body, the less it will distract you.)

Integrate your experience. Reflecting on experiences helps you notice what works, reap more learning and benefits, and motivate yourself to keep practicing. A few good options: pausing to notice how you feel, journaling, and sharing with a friend. (Writing and reflection suggestions are included with each practice area to help you do this.)

Find support. These practices emphasize things you can do on your own, and can themselves be a powerful source of support. Still, for many of us, it's immensely helpful to have additional support as we explore new experiences and aim to cultivate a consistent practice, to help us overcome obstacles and celebrate our accomplishments.

This support might come from a friend, a group or class, a workbook, or an online program. Consider what has worked for you in the past, and what would serve you now. It might be as simple as keeping a log to note when you have done a practice—perhaps combined with a reward if you do it consistently. If you have a buddy, you can call or text when you've done something, share photos, have a weekly lunch date, or reach out for support if you need it.

The poems in this collection offer another readily-available source of support. They emerged from intimate encounters with nature, Spirit, and creativity, and may inspire your own explorations of that terrain. Try reading a poem to spark your own writing, drawing, or creative movement, or as you delve into one of the practices. Reading it out loud or multiple times may increase the impact.

Practices for Connecting with Nature

"It's all alive. It's all connected. It's all intelligent. It's all relatives."
—*Bioneers*

"Those who dwell... among the beauties and mysteries of the Earth are never alone or weary of life."
—*Rachel Carson*

Many of us are drawn to be in nature, and for good reason. It awakens our senses and lifts our spirits. It helps us think better, feel better, work better, and heal better. The effects are so powerful that even a single plant in a room, a nature image on a wall, or a view of trees through a window has significant impacts.

And this is not just about our personal health and happiness. Contact with nature also helps us live in peace and balance, by making us more flexible, cooperative, and creative.

Even when we're not very present, being in nature restores and heals us. Yet when we slow down and pay attention, we can receive so much more. We see more beauty, feel more awe and delight, and experience more profound peace.

When we give it a chance, the natural world can speak to us very deeply. It reminds us that we are never alone, but part of a vast family of beings who are all potential friends and teachers. It connects us with immense reserves of living wisdom and creativity and activates our own intuitive intelligence. And it helps us remember who we are and why we're here.

For millennia, indigenous cultures have recognized the wisdom and sacredness of nature and their role in protecting it for future generations. Through both spiritual beliefs and daily customs, they fostered reverence and balance in their relations with the natural world. They knew their survival depended on this—as does ours.

When we listen to nature, when we open our hearts to its wisdom, we are inspired to walk more gently on the Earth, to treat "other" beings with love and respect, and to protect what we love. Through both small and large acts, each of us can help weave a web of respectful relations with all beings. Together, we can create a more Earth-honoring culture that honors and benefits all life.

The following practices are adapted from *Poems of Earth and Spirit: 70 Poems and 40 Practices for Deepening Your Connection with Nature,* which includes many more tips for both wild places and everyday life.

1. **Start where you are.** Notice how the natural world is part of your everyday life, even in the midst of a city—in food and water, plants and animals, daily and seasonal cycles, your own body, and more. Simply bringing more awareness to the presence of nature around you will strengthen your connection with it.

2. **Open your senses.** Your senses are gateways to the natural world, and when they are open you can experience it more fully. Practice tuning into your senses one at time, savoring the sights, sounds, scents, textures, and perhaps even flavors of nature. Closing your eyes will heighten your experience of other senses. Enjoy the music of birdsong or leaves whispering in the wind. Explore varied textures with your hands, bare feet, or your whole body. Or get to know a tree, flower, or small patch of Earth using all your senses. (While our culture emphasizes five key senses, we are gifted with many more ways of sensing and intuitively knowing.)

3. **Slow down.** Discover the power of the pause. When you're out for a walk, take time to stop, look, and listen, for a moment, a minute, or more. Gently explore an intriguing spot at a very leisurely pace— you may be amazed to find how much beauty and magic can exist in one small area. If you're ready for a deeper dive into stillness, sit quietly and simply be present in one place, bathing in the sights and sounds of nature. Or lie down, let your mind and body release into the support of the Earth, and practice the quietly radical art of resting. When you slow down or stop, new worlds can open up to you.

4. **Be present.** When you're truly present in nature, you're more available to receive the abundant gifts that await you. As you enter a natural setting, take a few moments to notice where you are and give yourself a chance to arrive. Sit or stand quietly and open your awareness to what's around you. Enjoy a few deep breaths, feel your feet on the Earth, and sense yourself landing in your body and in that place.

   As you move through a landscape, practice bringing mindful awareness to your surroundings and your experience in the moment. Notice what draws your attention and lean in for a closer look. See how fully present you can be with a single leaf, a flowing creek, or the warmth of sun on your skin.

5. **Go beyond words.** When we experience something exquisite, we often instinctively become quiet because it allows us to receive more fully. Being quiet is one of the simplest and best ways to notice and appreciate the many wonders of the natural world. The next time you're out, exercise

171

your right to remain silent, at least for part of the time. Tune into your surroundings and let nature speak to you. Notice what calls to you, and where you feel drawn to go (or stop). See if you can listen not just with your ears, but at a deeper level with your body, heart, and spirit.

Going solo makes it easier to be quiet and fully present with the peace and beauty of nature. Enjoy a solo walk or sit in a place where you feel comfortable. Or when you're out with other humans, invite them to try being quiet or going solo for a while and then share about your experiences. See how far you can go when you go beyond words.

6. **Make friends.** Making friends with "other" beings and natural places is easier than you may think. It starts with realizing it is possible and giving it a chance. Notice which beings or places you are instinctively drawn to, and find opportunities to connect with them, preferably one on one. Sit quietly with them, touch them, speak and listen to them—even a simple "hello" or "thank you" can establish a stronger bond. Tend the connection as you might with human friends or romantic interests. You may be surprised to discover the depth of love and friendship that can blossom.

7. **Give thanks.** Nature offers us many gifts—both tangible ones like food, water, and shade, and less tangible ones like peace, healing, and inspiration. Expressing gratitude helps us enjoy and cherish these gifts more. Try saying "thank you" to some of the beings and elements that give to you—naming names is good! You might pause to give thanks for a sunset, a lovely flower, or the food in your lunch.

Consider giving back to a special place by making an offering, removing trash, or volunteering. (See writing question 3.)

Writing and Reflection Suggestions

1. **"When I Am Among the Trees"** is the title of a poem by Mary Oliver. In your mind's eye, recall a time when you were "among the trees." Imagine you are there and use this as a springboard to write about your own experience. You also can adapt this prompt to reflect on your experience among other aspects of nature: when I am among the flowers, when I'm at the ocean...

2. **Write (or speak) as an aspect of nature.** Call to mind a being or element in nature that you feel a kinship with—perhaps a river, tree, or an animal—and see and feel them with you. Or go out into a natural setting, notice what calls to you, and tune into your connection with that being or element. In either case, feel their essence in your body and your bond with them, and let your body find a stance or movement in response. Explore that embodied experience for as long as you like, and then write or speak in the first person ("I am... ") as that being or aspect of nature.

3. **Write a letter to the Earth.** Write a hand-written love letter or thank-you letter to the Earth, or to a being in the natural world that is special to you. This may feel awkward at first, but if you give it a chance you may be surprised by how rewarding it can be. Allow yourself to feel your love and gratitude, and let them pour out on to the page. You may want to write in a natural setting or near your loved one, and read your letter out loud when

173

you're done. Consider sharing it with a trusted friend, or inviting them to write one of their own.

4. **Write your vows to the Earth.** Create personal vows expressing your love and commitment to the Earth, or to a being or place in nature that is meaningful to you. Write by hand and in a peaceful, natural setting if you can. Let yourself drop into your heart and your deepest intentions for this relationship. Give voice to your commitments to love, honor, cherish, and protect the Earth. Again, you might want to share this experience or what you write with a friend.

Practices for Connecting with Spirit

"God is too big to fit into one religion."
—*bumper sticker*

"The miracle is not to walk on water. The miracle is to walk on the green Earth in the present moment, to appreciate the peace and beauty that are available now."
—*Thich Nhat Hanh*

Humans have an innate longing to connect with something greater than ourselves. We might find this through a loving partner, a community, a path of service, or Spirit as we understand it. Whatever we believe, a direct relationship with Spirit is always available, and cultivating it can profoundly enrich our lives.

Although our bond with Spirit is innate and natural, the paths to accessing it aren't always obvious. The Spirit world is inherently intangible and mysterious, and too often humans further obscure it with confusing and contradictory messages about what Spirit is or isn't supposed to be. Fortunately, there are many ways to connect with the sacred, including through meditation, prayer, chanting, ceremony, and being in nature.

The freedom to explore practices that are meaningful for us is vital, especially if we've had negative experiences with a particular religious or spiritual path in the past. Regardless of our history, a healthy, fulfilling relationship with Spirit is always possible—just as if we've been hurt in one romantic partnership, we can go on to have a loving relationship with a different person.

How do we know when we are touching the sacred? There is no clear-cut answer, but many of us can sense when it happens. We may experience profound peace, awe, or oneness; feel a powerful heart opening, or receive guidance or creative inspiration that seems to originate from something greater than ourselves.

The following practices include many cross-cultural elements, and they are designed to be accessible to people with diverse beliefs—even those who wouldn't identify as spiritual. You can deepen any practice by slowing down, allowing space, connecting with your heart, directly invoking the Spirit, and/or being as fully present as you can.

1. **Notice what works for you.** There are many paths to Spirit. Exploring different practices and noticing when you feel connected with something greater than yourself will help you find yours. This may happen when you are alone or with others, silent or speaking a prayer, sitting still or moving mindfully. It may occur quickly, or more gradually over time. For many people, being in nature offers a simple and direct pathway to the sacred.

2. **See Spirit in you and around you.** Sometimes seeing is believing. Visualizing anything, including your relationship with Spirit, helps make it so—especially if you do it regularly. You can find an image that affirms your personal connection with Spirit by sensing into what that might look like, or by asking that an image come to you. It may appear in nature, or through prayer, meditation, a dream, or a work of art. Guided meditations or shamanic journeys also can help you find sacred images.

   Alternatively, you can try holding an image in your mind and heart and see if it resonates with you or sparks another image. Here are a few possibilities: a vertical column of light or energy connecting you with heaven and Earth, light or energy radiating out from your crown or heart, Spirit guides gathered around you, or yourself in a place where you experienced the presence of Spirit in the past.

3. **Tend the relationship.** Try relating to the Spirit as you might a close friend who loves you unconditionally. Be on speaking terms. Communicate directly, daily if possible, in ways that feel authentic. This may be quite simple and informal, like saying good morning or goodnight. Sometimes it is helpful to communicate with specific spirit guides, allies, or ancestors. At other times, you may want to connect with the Spirit realm more generally. In either case, calling on them regularly will strengthen the bond—as will expressing gratitude through words or offerings.

4. **Practice meditation and mindfulness.** Meditation is not merely a powerful way to calm the mind and reduce stress. It also cultivates the inner quiet and spaciousness that open the door to communion with Spirit. Even if your mind is busy and the moments of stillness few and far between, the practice of repeatedly returning to mindful awareness of the present moment will build your capacity to connect deeply—with Spirit and in all areas of your life.

There are many ways to meditate or be meditative. In addition to diverse traditions of seated meditation, you can explore walking meditation, yoga, qigong, chanting, or being quiet and present in nature. All have powerful benefits, as does practicing mindfulness during any activity—eating, washing dishes, driving, talking with your partner...

5. **Speak your own prayers and blessings.** There is great power in traditional prayers that have been spoken for millennia, as well as those that come through spontaneously and from the heart. Explore praying in whatever way is authentic for you—it may be as simple as addressing the spirit world and asking for help or giving thanks. You may want to speak blessings for beloved trees, humans, or other creatures. ("May you be..." and "may you have..." are lovely ways to seed a blessing.) With practice, this will feel more natural and you will hone your ability to readily connect with Spirit through your words.

6. **Make an offering or altar.** An offering is a beautiful and symbolic way to honor a special being, place, or spirit guide. It might be flowers, a stone, a song, a poem, or anything that is meaningful to you. Place or release your offering with intention, maybe as part of a ceremony (see below). Or you can create an altar by choosing special items that represent the sacred directions or qualities you wish to invoke and arranging them with care and reverence. Allow your intuition and the materials to guide you. (If you gather or place items in a natural setting, please be mindful of your impact.)

7. **Create a ceremony.** Ceremonies are an ancient and potent language for invoking the sacred, affirming what is true, and requesting support—especially when they are conducted with deep intention and presence. They may be simple or complex, spontaneous or planned, done on your own or with others. You can dedicate them to yourself, another person or being, or a place.

The basic elements are a clear intention, an opening and closing of ceremonial space, and other symbolic actions, all of which can be simple and intuitive. Below are a few examples. Feel free to start small—any one of these elements can be a ceremony in itself.

Opening options: lighting a candle, burning sage, crossing a threshold, making an altar, meditating, singing, drumming, rattling, thanking the land, setting an intention; or invoking the directions, ancestors, and/or Spirit guides and asking for support.

Options for core of ceremony: symbolic acts of clearing, release, transformation, healing, blessing, or thanksgiving. These might include washing, burning, planting seeds, burying, releasing into water, speaking or singing words, or dancing.

Closing options: a song, words of gratitude, gesture of integrating or letting go, thanking and releasing spirit guides, or crossing back over threshold.

It's wise to transition gently and mindfully out of ceremonial space. This may include being quiet, sitting still, lying down, moving gently, drinking water, eating, journaling, and/or sharing a few words.

Writing and Reflection Suggestions

1. **I see or sense the presence of the Spirit in...**

2. **I feel connected to something greater than myself when...**

3. **Write a letter to yourself in the voice of a wise and powerful entity**—perhaps the Earth, the Universe, Spirit, or your Higher Power. In the letter, allow this entity to express what is special about you, what they love about you, why you have been given the life and the lessons you have, and their deepest hopes and aspirations for you.

This can be especially valuable if you are feeling isolated or facing big challenges. Another option is to speak out loud in the voice of the wise entity.

Practices for Cultivating Natural Creativity

"All creation is co-creation."
—Marcia Conner

"If you can walk, you can dance; if you can talk, you can sing."
—saying from Zimbabwe

All living beings are naturally creative—including you! Humans are born to create, just as we are born to love. However, many of us don't see ourselves as creative because we don't regularly make art or music. Yet we express our creativity in myriad ways, including through everyday tasks like solving problems, parenting children, improvising meals, and creating beauty in our homes.

Creativity flows when we are open to inspiration and ideas and allow them to move through us freely. Saying "yes" to this flow, even in small ways, connects us with Source, honors our gifts, and brings joy and vitality into our lives.

Even if we don't produce anything tangible, or if what we produce is not particularly "good" according to our own or others' standards, we benefit from expressing ourselves creatively. Yes, there are real differences in talent and skill, but that doesn't mean that only the most gifted among us deserve to make art or music, or to be seen and heard. We all have a right to create and to share the fruits of our creation.

For most of us who aspire to be more creative, the essential ingredients are not more training or talent, but rather safety, freedom, and encouragement—to try new things, to follow our instincts and ideas, and even to make mistakes or (gasp!) to fail. We can give ourselves this space and permission, or receive them from friends, teachers, groups, or the natural world.

The following practices are crafted for people who want to overcome challenges to creative flow, yet also may be helpful to those who are comfortable with creative expression.

1. **Notice how you are already creative.** Humans express creativity in diverse ways, including through seemingly mundane activities like getting dressed or making a sandwich. Simply bringing more awareness to these varied creative outlets can nurture your creativity and self-esteem. Bonus: find easy opportunities to bring a bit more color and flair into your daily life— wear a bright scarf, sing in the car, or make a small bouquet. (See writing question 3.)

2. **Feed your creativity.** Notice which people, places, and activities feed your creativity, and regularly nourish yourself with them. These may include free time, solitude, particular music, dancing, or being in nature. Also tune into your creative rhythms, including the times of the day or week when you are more creative, and build that into your plans when possible. You might write early in the morning or sing on Sunday evenings. (See writing suggestions 1 and 2.)

3. **Be in nature.** The natural world inspires creativity like nothing else, and there are many ways to access this inspiration. You may want to write, draw, or do other creative work in a natural setting, or soon after returning from one. You can actively co-create with nature by being open and receptive, tuning into your surroundings, and seeing what wants to come through. Or bring a question or intention out into a natural setting, ask for guidance, and then sit still or wander quietly and notice what draws your

attention and what ideas come to you. Writing down what you receive and/or sharing it with someone will help you integrate your experience.

4. **Keep it simple.** If you don't see yourself as highly creative or have fears around creativity (which includes almost all of us!) doing something easy and without a specific outcome in mind will help your inner critic stand down. Engage in "child's play" like coloring, doodling, making rubbings, or other projects that you enjoyed as a child or with your own kids. Play with watercolors or clay without trying to make something specific—just give yourself space to explore and see what emerges organically. Or do a creative project that has an intended outcome but is still easy and enjoyable for you, like making a collage, stringing beads, creating a beautiful salad, or arranging stones into patterns.

5. **Go play!** Play with kids. Play with dogs. Play in the sprinklers. Play in the snow. Play with sand, water, mud, or leaves—extra points for getting wet or dirty! Play a simple game like seeing how long you can keep a ball up in the air. Get out of your head and into the moment. If you're out of practice with playing, dogs and young children are excellent teachers.

6. **Let yourself be moved.** Allowing your body to move spontaneously and intuitively helps you connect with your authentic self and activate creativity. Here is one way to do that: Go to a place in nature where you are comfortable, either on your own or with someone you feel safe with. Find an intriguing spot and quietly tune into your surroundings and what you are sensing in the moment. Notice what captures your attention in a

pleasing way, perhaps leaves moving in the breeze or water flowing. Rest your awareness on that, drinking in the sights, sounds, and sensations. Then allow some movement to arise in your own body and unfold organically. Enjoy letting a tree, a stream, or the ocean inspire your movement.

7. **Journal—just for you.** Writing regularly in a journal is one of the best ways to nurture your connection with yourself and creativity. Write by hand and from the heart, every day if you can. Give yourself freedom to be messy and imperfect, and to write whatever you want without a sense that someone is looking over your shoulder. To help make this safe, keep your journal private or be very selective about how you share it.

   Consider what type of journal will meet your needs. It might be a simple notebook that reduces pressure to write "well," a visually beautiful journal that inspires you, and/or something compact enough to easily carry along. You may want to have several journals dedicated to different purposes, like recording nature experiences or dreams. Creating a designated space for something is a good way to invite it into your life.

Writing and Reflection Suggestions

1. **I feel creative when...**

2. **When I want to get inspired, I...**

3. **My creativity reveals itself in many ways, both large and small. These include...**

Make a list and describe each one briefly. Be generous in giving yourself credit for as many signs of creativity as you can, including seemingly small and ordinary ones. See if you can come up with at least 10 or 20.

4. **My creativity is like...**
Complete the sentence with one of the following, and then write about it: the sun, the moon, a seed, a flower, a tree, a mountain, a river—or any wild animal or aspect of nature that calls to you. You may want to repeat one prompt multiple times, write about more than one, or speak out loud rather than writing. Afterwards, reflect on what you have learned about the nature of your creativity.

5. **Write a permission slip giving yourself plenty of space to nurture and express your creativity.**
Describe why your creativity is important, why it needs freedom to come through, and what that looks like. Write spontaneously and from the heart; and read your permission slip out loud when you're done. You may want to post it where you can see it, re-read it periodically, or share it with a trusted friend.

Last Words

Many Thanks!

This book is the work of many hands—and also paws, wings, branches, and blossoms. Literally thousands of beings helped make it possible. I am grateful to them all and will name some here…

The trees, plants, animals, and other more-than-human beings who invited me into a larger flow of creation and freely shared their wisdom and inspiration.

Special places in the wild that kept calling me back, especially the North Coast of Santa Cruz, Rancho Del Oso, the Big Sur Coast, the Yuba River, and Kings Canyon. Thank you for always giving me what I needed and so much more.

The spirit guides and allies who support me more than I will ever know, even when I forget they are there.

The Vajrapani Institute for the many blessings of silent retreat and the opportunity to receive the gifts that come only in stillness, including numerous poems.

Ilan Shamir for the deliciously personal and poetic foreword, and for reflecting the essence of my work so graciously.

Mária Kersey for clearly reflecting the spirit of these poems through her exquisite drawings, generously donating her time and artistic talent, taking the author photo, and giving 30 years of loving friendship.

Mary Reynolds Thompson for helping me become a woman of fewer words, expert advice on myriad aspects of writing and publishing, and superhuman displays of editing prowess.

Those who reviewed or proofed sections of text: Alan
Voegtlen, Andrew Davis, Carroll LaFleur, Greg
Thrush, Jared Jones, Jay Siedenburg, Jill Doneen,
Joanna Jarvis, Joel Wallock, Mitchell Goldstein, Nina
Siedenburg, and Tamara Myers. Thank you for helping
me see the good and make needed repairs.

Terry Teitelbaum for heroically solving eleventh-hour
formatting glitches that had stumped the official tech
support staff and almost made me pull my hair out.

Jeremy Thornton for the gorgeous cover design and
Ian Woolcock for the stunning cover image.

The "Circle of Friends" who believed in this project
and helped fund the initial publication costs. (See list
on next page.)

Everyone who has told me about how my poems or
practices have touched your life. Your reflections have
lifted my spirits and helped me to continue walking this
path even when it became rocky. (Gentle reader, if you
have been inspired by an artist's work, I encourage you
to let them know!)

Ariana Candell for being a steady, supportive friend
and a generous creative collaborator, and for doing
more than anyone else I know to help my poems reach
appreciative audiences.

Other friendly mammals who supported me and this
project in diverse ways:
    Suzanne Morrow for inviting me to her land to
listen, write, and restore myself.
    Megan Hawk for complementing my poems with
her beautiful Native American flute music at live
events.

Heather Houston and the women of Yala Lati for the joy of lifting our voices in harmony.

The Dance Church community for getting me out of my head and into my body, and for being a warm and welcoming tribe.

My furry friend Riley, for her ready purr and reminding me to cuddle and play every day.

Everyone who has loved me, believed in me, and encouraged me (fortunately too numerous to list here!)

And anyone else I should have acknowledged here but didn't, my heartfelt thanks!

Finally, a deep bow of gratitude to all my ancestors for making it possible for me to be here, and to my parents, who have given me so much. I couldn't have done it, or anything, without you.

Circle of Friends for *Space Between the Stones*

Ariana Candell
Carroll LaFleur
Cindy Mitchell
Claire Murphy
Connie Habash
Dave and Mary Anne
   Kramer-Urner
Donna Scheifler
Erin Ramsden
Jared Jones
Jennifer Alexander
Joanna Jarvis
Kris Ayer
Krista Holt
Laura Sera

Linda Munn
Livia Hartgrove
Louise and Joel
   Wallock
Marcia Heinegg
Mária Kersey
Megan Hawk
Mitchell Goldstein
Shari Rose
Susan and Steve
   Kauffman-
   Lustgarden
Tamara Myers
(plus six anonymous
donors)

About the Author

Kai Siedenburg is a nature connection guide, Ecotherapist, and poet who is passionate about helping people connect with the healing power of nature for the benefit of all beings. A pioneer in integrating nature awareness and mindfulness as a path to mind-body wellness, she offers individual sessions, group programs, and consulting services through Our Nature Connection.

Her approach is rooted in deep listening to nature and shaped by what activist Carolyn Casey calls "a willingness to collaborate with everything." It also is informed by 30-plus years of experience developing innovative educational programs, and by extensive practice in mindfulness, holistic healing, and creative expression. Kai's life and work are woven around four golden threads: love for people, love for the Earth, desire for deep connection, and a strong call to contribute.

She lives on the ancestral lands of the Awaswas people (now represented by the Amah Mutsun Tribal Band), where the mountains meet the sea in Santa Cruz, California. Kai loves to find herself out on the Earth, in her garden, in water, or on the dance floor, and aspires to touch the Earth with her hands or bare feet every day.

Space Between the Stones is Kai's second book. She is also the author of *Poems of Earth and Spirit: 70 Poems and 40 Practices to Deepen Your Connection with Nature*.

Learn more about her story at
OurNatureConnection.com

About the Illustrator

Mária Kersey is an artist and public high school teacher based in Santa Cruz, California. Childhood experiences exploring the outdoors seeded her lifelong love of nature. Summer camping trips with her parents and brother inspired her to continue these adventures as a young adult with solo excursions backpacking in British Columbia and camping in Arizona. Later, as a mom and teacher, she hiked the Sierras with her sons and organized photography trips to Yosemite for her students. Being in nature enriches her life and relationships with family and friends—including the author of this book.

Mária began her artistic career as an apprentice potter at eleven years old, taught ceramics as a teenager, and later earned a degree in graphic design with a focus on illustration. She creates with diverse materials and modes, including woodworking, construction, drafting, tile masonry, photography, gardening, ceramics, painting, drawing, computer graphics, singing, and playing acoustic music. On her days off from teaching, she works for the local California State Parks.

About TreeSisters

Imagine a reforestation revolution ignited by the shared creativity and courage of a global network of millions of women.

TreeSisters is a non-profit organization aiming to radically accelerate tropical reforestation by engaging the unique feminine consciousness, gifts, and leadership of women everywhere and focusing it towards global action.

TreeSisters are planting over a million trees a year, and they are now calling for women to plant a billion trees a year, by becoming a treesister and contributing monthly to tropical reforestation.

Sales of this book raise funds in aid of TreeSisters (3% of total proceeds before expenses).

TreeSisters.org

About Our Nature Connection

Our Nature Connection inspires people to connect directly and mindfully with nature as a path to greater peace, joy, and healing in their lives and in the world.

We empower people to:
- Find simple ways to connect with the Earth in daily life,
- Cultivate intimate and nourishing bonds with wild places and more-than-human beings, and
- Access nature-based healing for mind, body, and spirit.

Our work is a gentle yet powerful integration of deep nature connection, mindfulness practice, and holistic healing—a unique approach we call *NatureWise*.

We offer a wealth of practices appropriate for diverse settings, and share them through group programs, individual sessions, consulting services, and the written word.

OurNatureConnection.com

Resources for Connecting with Nature

OurNatureConnection.com
Visit our website for poetry and articles that bring you closer to nature and nature closer to you. Sign up to receive monthly infusions of nature-based goodness.

Turning Toward Nature (home-based program)
Learn how to deepen your connection with nature wherever you are through this four-week course, which combines engaging group calls with easy, enjoyable nature-based activities. Includes options for both cities and wild places, and for one-on-one support.

Group Nature Immersion Programs
Discover what it's like to connect more intimately and mindfully with the natural world, and what becomes possible when you do that. Leave feeling relaxed and replenished, with simple tools you can use to connect with nature anytime, anywhere.

Individual Sessions
Face life's challenges with greater clarity and ease through skilled, personalized support. Learn how to receive healing and guidance from the natural world and activate your innate wisdom and creativity. (Available via phone, Zoom, Skype, or in person.)

Consulting Services
Enliven and empower your professional work by tapping into nature's capacity to calm, heal, and inspire—outdoors, indoors, and even on Zoom! We can teach you simple yet potent practices to share with clients, help you design innovative individual or group sessions, or craft a custom program to meet your goals.

Learn more at OurNatureConnection.com

Also Available from Our Nature Connection

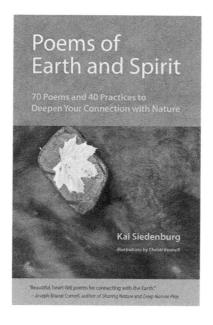

At turns peaceful, playful, and provocative, *Poems of Earth and Spirit* is a collection of poetry and practices that draws us into deeper kinship with all life. Through intimate original poems, we feel what it's like to walk on padded paws, to take wing, to root ourselves in the Earth. And through carefully crafted practices, we learn how to cultivate a direct connection with nature that supports and sustains us wherever we go.

"Beautiful, heart felt poems for connecting with the Earth."

—Joseph Bharat Cornell, author of *Sharing Nature* and *Deep Nature Play*

"These inspiring poems and simple practices will help you deepen your connection with nature wherever you are."

—Mary Reynolds Thompson, author of *Reclaiming the Wild Soul*

2020 Next Generation Indie Book Awards Finalist

PoemsofEarthandSpirit.com

Made in the USA
Monee, IL
02 July 2022